Diary of a Man

Daniel J. Crowley

TRAFFORD
PUBLISHING

Note for Librarians: A cataloguing record for this book is available from Library and Archives
Canada at www.collectionscanada.ca/amicus/index-e.html
ISBN 1-4120-7550-5

*Printed in Victoria, BC, Canada. Printed on paper with minimum 30% recycled fibre. Trafford's print shop
runs on "green energy" from solar, wind and other environmentally-friendly power sources.*

TRAFFORD
PUBLISHING™

Offices in Canada, USA, Ireland and UK

This book was published *on-demand* in cooperation with Trafford Publishing. On-demand
publishing is a unique process and service of making a book available for retail sale to the
public taking advantage of on-demand manufacturing and Internet marketing. On-demand
publishing includes promotions, retail sales, manufacturing, order fulfilment, accounting and
collecting royalties on behalf of the author.

Book sales for North America and international:
Trafford Publishing, 6E–2333 Government St.,
Victoria, BC V8T 4P4 CANADA
phone 250 383 6864 (toll-free 1 888 232 4444)
fax 250 383 6804; email to orders@trafford.com
Book sales in Europe:
Trafford Publishing (UK) Limited, 9 Park End Street, 2nd Floor
Oxford, UK OX1 1HH UNITED KINGDOM
phone 44 (0)1865 722 113 (local rate 0845 230 9601)
facsimile 44 (0)1865 722 868; info.uk@trafford.com
Order online at:
trafford.com/05-2445

10 9 8 7 6 5 4 3

Words spoken—
  thru the written pages of beauty
caressed and aligned
  in the heart
illuminating out of presence
  with expression of spirit and passion
challenged, addressed, divided
  and faced with truth
"reflecting" the soul, with whispers
  of verse and rhyming means
    love, love and the dire to be...

along this road traveled, written and read
  the words, the music that's weaved,
threaded and connected
between and within
  the essence of life
upon the death
  we all face
the beauty –
  perplex and simplified
with the stories that give us name
  and make us dream beyond our reality
  "creative and enlightened"
thru the pain, adversity and the struggles
  of everyday life
I write to explore –
  not just for myself but to illuminate within
    yourself
    that freedom and faith
sharing in the experience thru the dusk of
day and arising upon the transcendent
colors of dawn

in a greeting peace across the horizon
of self reflection
tranquil and soothing
one within us all
so different yet the same!

The Door Way

lets cast out the memories
and fulfill the dreams
escape the mind
and heal the heart
with depth of soul

igniting daylight passions
and the mystic
of nights ebbing flow
burning into the flames
of midnight
stars and moonlit skies
half – mast'd
in death and birth

speeding highways
cross country roads
listen, listen in wit
to the presence,
to the harmony
through the blowing winds
of time
and the mistakes made
upon love and faith learned
open the door
and enter the escape,
the reality of being.
relinquish the ties
the parallel lines
of division
and be...

The Opening

sit me at the edge
of the river
beside its still lake
and strip me naked
till I'm free, free
of this pain
slip me into the sunset
and dress me warm,
warm with your love
upon the stars ecstasy
rippling in the dark,
light mass
and let me embody,
embody the beauty,
the gentleness
of its presence
there within its sweet kiss,
kiss of grace
half lit upon the dreams fuel
of erotic mid-night
savoring the fugitive
of words
immaculately feeling, touching
the hush of desire
upon the shooting stars,
stars gleam
slowly introducing
the essence,
the essence of passionate love
to the encircling depth

of color,
color arising in the belly
and shadow,
shadow of the hearts
infinite ache

and here I sit, in the aspiration

viewing the silence and dew,
dew of the morning's light

opening

*This is a tribute to a singer, a poet,
an inspiration, who broke thru to
the other side- Jim Morrison*

The Poet

death alights the night
awoken to the dream
past and present
and
left in division

an alcohol twitch
stirred in the flowing veins
of thought and reason
born into the calculus
destination
alive, with fire and mystic
torn and twisted
blatant and intelligent
upon the growing presence
of song and lyric
dancing, singing
on the edge,
the edge of life
screaming passionate vocation
ripping, tearing the means to an end
open and free to the brilliance
of democracy
on a sexual voyence
of cinematic reality
lived, pillaged and bleed
with words,
words

of a voice, timelessly
enfaced
loved and hated!
the beauty, the beast
of lament
pushing beyond-
Sunset Blvd., Venice Beach
Los Angeles
State and Grove, Laurel Canyon
New Haven, Miami,

Paris

the end,

dressed in words
un-understanding, my friend
dancing to the beginning
the one conversed shared vision,
the end
in light now shining
the beauty, the peace
singing ode,
the poet, the singer
the man, the legend
down on love street
changing from sad
to gladness
in a weeping world,
wild and unwed
full and empty
to what,
to what you,
you can't comprehend.

❖ cafe nine
❖ entangle-ment ❖ the city-walk
❖ symmetry ❖ reflections
❖ a poetic-kiss ❖ my sanctuary
❖ the composition of...
❖ the cascading breath ❖ the jeweled veil
❖ love at the end of the sun
❖ spring's blossom ❖ the giving
❖ flesh, soothing flesh
❖ sea of beauty

Café Nine

I'm not here to oppose war
and political martyrs or masters
just the unanswered voice
in your head
the injustice of yourself to be
with good reason
to challenge and be wed
the contrast, the distance
between and within
like Oscar Wilde said
it's when people tend to
agree with me that I tend to think
I am not right
and when they don't I just,
just might be

upon social society
and it's plastic means
there in the fruit
of the tree's and the temptation
Kerry, Bush
the hate, the truth
power and greed
a consciousness,
a vision
following the dream
and the freedom
expressive heart
of dire and faith
upon the limitless breath
of dance
not lead,

but inspired, enlived
to the call of each,
not of consensus
but to the hearth
which is neither wrong nor right but
present to,
to it's integrity.

ancient and modern
beyond a call of society

but divine in heart
and true to name
politics in face
of the beloved
in the reflection of you
in the reflection of me
death and war
rage!
beauty in the beast
the terror of yourself
the truth,
the truth
in kneeling depth
underlying
the eyes view
T.V., media
can you see,
can you see

into the stars and stripes
of your own soul
the truth,
answers

Entanglement

weaved in the feast,
the forest of the heart
time expands and collapses
from the beast and beauty
of love,
and unity
enabled and revealed
through one's own evolution
born and accepted
in the courage to be
alive
truly in the passage
of the moment
present and manifested
beyond the religion,
profoundly -
in soul
to the calling of
oneness
embraced and kissing
the freedom

from the politics,
of being human.

The City walk

Jaded streets of vision
laughter in the corner
an old man wearing
the flesh of a young mans
passion
sunlight through the darkness
of the mind,
crowds
the dreams,
the conversations
drawing, escaping,
the emptiness
and pain
downtown angels
in the city,
the city of New, New
Haven
groans and beggars
weep,
the songs, the fear,
the sanity –
of its surrounding walls
esteeming beauty, beauty
broken and perfected

and the children
of time-
whisper, whisper
by the sidewalks,
the halls, the church's,
the educated steeples

of conformity

in and out
of blood and illusion
media and the painted
prices
of reframe
the disciples,
selling,
being

the masked martyrs
of faith
delivering, delivering

"the message"
in the streets,
deprived and shadowing
the soul,
the soul of
translation
a verse of words
headlining
the birth,
the birth
of corporation!
bleeding universal means,
numbers, numbers,
numbers
severing the humanness,
from the footsteps of dawn

Symmetry

In the corners, the passion
of love
"tiny dancers and butterfly kisses"
sing upon the senses,
the heart of walls
awakened through
a wavering bliss

"time and moment"

her beauty long imbues
a depth,
a distance
broken and amend
to a pearl inside
a shell
there freedom lies
innocent and ageless
hidden and naked
in the city lights
where the crowds amass
and you stand alone
present, to your own
in complement
thru the world around
stripped and unbroken
like a sonnet, a poem
and the singers' soul
of destiny

the love of yourself

and it's exposed
self-expression

embraced and open

to the face
of faceless love

a beauty wide-
and blossoming
conceived and reciprocated
through the eyes of each
other

Reflections

In the silence
of Sunday evenings stir
time alighted memories
set current past and dreaming
through the lone
vast veins
as the moon and shuffled speech
conjures the star lights engage
timid and voicing
beauty against the pain
songs and sunsets
painting romance
on the wings
of language

the arc within and between
sensuous and obsession
evil and good

a drink on the foil,
the border of self and meaning,
the night untold and turning
love, desire, fear
and its humility
to be...
broken,
naked and free
a sexual overture
of nothing
and everything
a stranger of urgency
and passion
becoming,
instinctively awoken
to the beauty, the essence
of emotion
toiled and tied
feeling real and pure,
the pleasure-pain

bittersweet

love,
sexuality!

A Poetic Kiss

her scent lingers in me
like the taste
of freedom
enchanting the deepest depth
of beauty voiced and given
transcending my appetite
and fever
to the peak of deliverance
here in the warming dream
and memory
flesh in flesh
the eye in soul conversation
speaks,
in literate silence
profoundly sung
and accentuated
in still moving breath
and vision
weaved in through and wedded
with savory grace
to the exotic artistry
of growing emotion
dressed and naked
to the kiss
still in presence
and pleasure
of her scent
our beauty,
in moment, in time
enraptured, un-relinquished
and facilitating upon the lips
of love

My Sanctuary

her soft eyes penetrate
and flourish
the depth,
the depth of beauty
unpretentious
and illuminant
to the wavering lights
flow
in the tinted room's
presence
grown, radiating through
and surrounding
deep, deep
in natural grace
eden and the goddess,
the lady of the lake
glances
daunting the eve of springs
blossom
rain, the rain outside
the window
falling, resonating
her willow
enlightened hair
colorful and bright
dancing aloft
her shoulders
in a glow,
piercing the essence,
the dreaming stigma
of a woman,
and her beauty

The Composition of...

I can feel the distance,
move,
move upon her slow sensuous dress
close and hesitant (pausing)
with a smile
and a patience of beauty
caressing in her eyes
the long silhouette
of youth
feeding the warmth, the pleasure
of the sun's light
morning, mid afternoon
still framed and dreaming
o' the hunger, the hunger
is in the streets,
upon the structure
the visionary means
cast in call,
sex and emotion
meet,
meet at the crosswalk
of desire dddesire...
the bedroom sheets
and the showers, showers of alleviation
weep within
its thrust, its thirst
of growing cries,
passionately in verse
and free
therein the sketches of beauty
ebbing thru the candlelight visions flow,

flow of sex
weaved and threaded
to and between

the hearts slow dark and light
enunciation
of face and reflection

my love, my lust
breathing, penetrating
the day,
the day into night

the heaven, the wavering songs
presence
delivering out and within,
within
her beauty

The Cascading Breath

The scent of smoke
arouses me
deep in the belly
of my breath
dancing off the presence
between
the early autumn eve
of night,
and the falling rain
curling me up
under the sheets
of sex, love and fantasy
incrementing as I breathe
the night in posse
of warming flesh
through the cool
spawning rain
dripping in a symphony,
a harmonizing procession
smiling
onto the meeting
lament,
erotic freedom
astir,
in the air,
the lungs of dream
amid the mystic myth darkness
in a slow draw
of seeping creation

the taste,
the erection
of night

raining scents
emerge
the moonlight stranger
the wilderness,
upon the forest feast
of tenderness
arms in rapture
behind the mask,
the vision
of what you believe

semen in the uterus
of the sky
whispers songs
in the ears
union of flesh and soul
spiritually embodied
fed and spoken
to the one shared breath

love alight, the moments
infused beauty

cascade
of dawn

broken, healed
and met

The Jeweled Veil

this is the night
awakened
to laughter,
see it spiral
out of the prism
of the dawn
out stretched across
the peaking horizon's color
this is not
darkness,
but the taste, the taste
of serenity
dressing the cauldron
of peace
drunk with the filaments,
the vast sky,
the moon rising in full
a consciousness
in the garden
alive with the muse,
in songs and scents
of the soul,
the soul's blissful
dance, dance
of light
interchanging the mirror
of the clouds
behind the jeweled veil
of stars
love, love's come and gone
and following

the passage, the shoreline
of crimson
through the slate
of air, breathing
words,
words of silence

stripped erotically
in flow
and escaping
the night
at the edge,
the beginning
a bleeding ecstasy
of the virgin,
the virgin's crossing youth
through the thighs
screaming petition
wet,
and stiff
to its waking

the waking sheets
of the unveiled
stains,
stains of the mystic
intricate primate smell, smell
of the night,
the night
in you

releasing!

Love at the End of the Sun

she does little things
to warrant me
whispers of darkness
screams of light
calling out in name
the dawn of passion
and sensuous taste
beauty,
awoken and taken face
peace
and the soothing tides
wave against the moon
at midnight, with sweet erection
and climax

love, love at the end
of the sun

picturesque and vision'd
the heart of song
zestful and dreamed
flowers in the gardens
enter in me

love, love at the end
of the sun

stirring the dance
alive and free
amid the eyes
entangled

upon the moon, the stars
into the twilight sky
between,
the heart and womb
of what warrants me
love, love at the end
of the sun
days before long hour nights
presence waits
in the dreaming tree
roots

love, love at the end
of the sun

un-contemptuous and pure
the flowing river
destine
and met
time
and moment
captured
and engaged

love, love at the end
of the sun

beauty,

awoken with a kiss
upon the arrival of one's

own faith
reborn in beauty's breath
therein the souls of two,
two in one
eating from its chosen
fruit

love, love at the end
of the sun

Spring's Blossom

awoken within her
feast of beauty
the day greets the night,
songs and expressions
a dance,
a celebration
of...
desire,
nipples,
tongues,
and lips
a fleshing forest
expanded
and explored
through the throttle
of gentle improvisation
touched
and
caressing
the silhouettes
imbue
changing, igniting
the look,
the feel,

"romance"

the windows
of soul,
souls engaging

depth!
faced and baring

the meadows,
the rain
falls
inducing lust
of spring

opening

blooming
vast
and present
to all that is
and all that
can be
two in climax,
climaxing
the wet,
subtle enfacement
sweating out
skin to skin
the enthrall
of beauty,
beauty,
beauty

The Giving

slithering mist
tainted and filled
the autumn bleeds
death, rebirth
a change of season
seeps and sings
if I had loved you less
you would have loved
me more
a change in face
reflection and depth
reaching in, crawling out
the morning after, the night before

the eve, halloween
a dark and mystic,
a vast openness
to belief, love and relation

changing color
beautiful and arrayed
rooted and masked
with life, new beginnings
speaking truth through
the bleeding veins of season
if I had loved you less
you would have loved me more
blossomed and blinded
the rage of image
changing, leading

face to face
with the growing sun
and rising moon
across the desert of time
and truth
love, love
the presence, the absence
there of...

Flesh, Soothing, flesh

soft and languid, the night
drifts into the paradise
of my veins
breaking the dawn
out from
within
the heart of the sunset
sinking and dancing
unto the beach shore waves,
waves that mediate against
the dream,
the dream in face
motionless and moving

the destination
whispers, whispers
across a changing horizon
still born and breathing
the taste, the taste
of beauty
violets erotic freedom
penetrates open
and vast
upon the silhouettes imbue,
imbuing youth

lust, a wilderness,
innocent, broken
and escaping
the city, the garden

of birth

the paradox bliss
of nothingness
seeping, seeping
with open embrace
colored
and alight
to emotion

the wanting end
through windows and walls
crooned and weeping,
its awakening

Sea of Beauty

turquoise –
her body wavering
like the sea

flesh and skin
beauty, beauty

in her,
I swim infinite
an infinite romance
upon the moonlight stars,
sloth and breaking
the morning horizons surf
of grace and presence
on the wings
dancing whispers,
alone and close
murmuring
the ache,
the fulfillment
deep and passionate
embryonic to the faceless,
faceless soul
alive
and
astounding
beauty, beauty

imperishable
beauty

concave and coeval
her body,
her eyes,
transcend, transcend
to my embrace

flowing soft and tender
beneath the imminent
surface
serenely, so serenely
expressed

"spoken"
wordlessly

wordlessly, expressing love
thru movement and stillness
of the moment

Time, Self and Space

my reaction begins to slow
and my mind howls
the churning feast
of the deadened growth
sickle and stern
to the birth,
the bleeding religion
of corporate stigma
soul and spirit
sucked and unwed to the vision

preacher in the alley

love, it's only love
tossed and turned
it's another day
down on the Blvd.
of Hollywood dreams
painted and paved
the smoke screen of words
unthreaded,
to its means
tears of the soul
screaming out the chitter chatter
of the streets
lost and educated
freedom with no moral
dancing in neon greed
speaking something they don't understand,
tears of the soul
screaming in its reins

pieces of eleven
as twelve strikes the clock

the lions in the den
and the lizards out of the cage
time, season
the hours growing near
destiny awaits the change
of day,
choice
and the mind baring pain
the prison of time

tears of the soul

screaming, screaming out reframe
truth, value
"humanness"
open the door

and speak, speak

redemption

3 Against 1

The night in young
bleeding off the roots
of season
autumns air crisp
and cool
a tangle of emotion stirs
in the stillness
of its innocence
deep behind the eyes
of birth
sings,
a procession
of something ugly, disheveled
in nature
born and breeding
through the lighted way
of vision
the cloud covered,
breaking quarter moon,
streets of the city's
ignorance
a cult, the crime
stealing language of soul
standing 3-3-3 against 1
just because,
just because
darkness has fallen
into the hearts, hiding
behind the face of a child
street lights crying

witness,
to the blood scar emotion
of the four letter word

H A T E

just because
just because

the raping coward ness
enfaced
turns the world and cheats
you and me

of what is freedom,
freedom
rage of prosecution
desecrated
just because,
just because

laughter in the thrill,
courage-less villain,
together
3-3-3 against 1
am I right or wrong

just because,
just because

blood on the night
skin vision
autumn's death bleeding colors

hang off the trees
beautiful and different,
one in the same
here in the streets
tied in emotion
lingering and captivating
life and the association there of...
the contrast between,
a faceless few
reckoning ignorance
and goodwill
just, just
because
broken, violated
hung in reframe,
hatred drawn and fed
like a needle to the vein
standing,

3-3-3 against 1

victim to the venom
the crucifix, the crucifix
of love
Jesus,
the children

3-3-3 against 1

forgive them,
the fraught nemesis

souls
tout in blindness
of the present, present day
of what is expression
and what is just plain, plain
ignorance!!!

Alchemy's Enfacement

child like in a playground
of youth
sitting in a distance
and wavering,
wavering through the sweet
forest breath
speaking, the spectrum
beneath the illusions depths,
flowers soiled
and rooted,
rooted amid the nourishment
absorbed

canyons and valleys
mountains and lakes
meeting,
meeting at the point,
the portraits succumbed
within the ocean's mass
the tumble, the religious
rights
and the curtains
faith
whisper and hum
beauty,
beauty from the storm
through the doors
of passage
and tragedy
of heart
the benign love
and breaking demise

shadowed and enthralled
transfixed and engaging
the meadows,
the meadows muse
and city's walls
scripted -
in writing
foretold in lore
ancient, timeless
fathers,
and goddesses
of the night
awake now,
awake
between the dawn
and darkness
the mystic wilderness
transcending,
transcending the birthplace,
the feast of the soul
and enter, enter
the palace, the fortress
of your freedom
experiencing its,
its reward

the lucid eyes of
embrace,
sing in festival
of three,
seven, four

Street Emotion

suicide blonde dressed
in street corner attention
lisp and mane
emotion
love's fix
and game
a hollow holiday
of whiskey and cocaine
a dire of soul
whispers out and in
strange days
the waiting sun
of darkness
city streetlights
neon bars, music flowing
in depth of beat
feel fix of emptiness
sings on the lips
a change from coldness
to bliss
alcohol moments
alight, laughter,
happiness
on the edge between
a jack and an ace of spades
latitudes of emotion,
thought
sweet Mary of night's emancipation
deep in prayer
choose the light
of your eyes

heaven and earth
suicide blonde and the kiss of reason
today is a new day,
a new year
empty your pockets,
shake the coat of emotion
and strip your soul
naked to the change of season

give birth, a dialectic of meaning
to the words inside your heart
born and now awakened
my beauty,
upon the streets
of hope

Dust and Dire

the insoluble beauty croons
the lilies of dawn
upon love's engaging call
destine and forgiven
linear and aroused
to the songs muse

swayed in heat
and cinematic vision

she dances with the night
received
tenderly soothing
the riot, the passion
of lips and flesh
a commencement of the sun
and tides racing moon
within the swimming sky of romance
tattooing, a memory
half knit shirt,
crescent and demurring
a fantasy, an ecstasy, a dance
of snake skin eyes
long and inflowing

beauty, beauty

the temptress, the ancestral guardian
emerging the divide

in heart, fertile and shining
the ancient and primal

honoring,

soul

beauty

tasted and perceived
prayed and awoken

beauty

Integrity

above the noise
of my confusion
life sits along the river

bed of roses, thorns
and ravens claws
beauty that's sharp, soft
and angry
poised and belligerent
growing in the age of death
and innocence
long embracing the umbilical cord
of truth and reason
swallowed in the prostitution
of the lamb
sacrificed and offered
blindness streaks through the eyes
of mass perception
drawing the lights and fame,
and the red carpet walkways
prepared for its slaughter
speaking, questioning
the media cuts and manes
in the foreplay of the news,
integrity

The City Song

walking in the eyes stare
of hunger, lust and greed
envy and jealousy

I in the phrase of love
question, search
in the fleshing warmth
of a woman
the soul of who
I am
upon the touch
aspiring unity and freedom
exploration and mystic
a step into the darkness
out on the edge
of the mornings depth
from the silence,
the peace of wisdom
between the contrast
of that which is
and that which
can be
night and day
light and darkness
faith,
and human doubt
arising in flow
aloft the winds of change
and its desire to be

love's presence
and denial

afraid and secure
distant and aware

the saddle in which I sit
untamed and inspired
for the journey
vigor'd and enlightened
captured and unseen

firelights of evil
and the colors array
of strength, therein
the silence
of dawn and the sunsets passion
in the heart
of presence
speaking,
the prayers resonance
of collective being

through the swords
of the devils tongue
in defiant to the belief
of something more
subtle and essential
of truth and reason

the eyes of fear
upon the city streets
deemed and un-awakened
your knight in shining
the goddess in gleam
fools of the present
awake in the past,

the duel is within
yourself
and the perception
is either your guide or enemy

the long walk twists
and turns
the gate, the abide
of the burning flame
destine
and self-destructed
for love calls
the eyesight of the soul

the lights are on
is anybody home?

The Mirrors Face in You

death's meeting me,
the gleam of the sun
the shadow of the moon
escaping,
the night's hold
and openness
of daylights shame
heaven and hell
wave in and out
of the veil between
the casting thoughts
and the faith held
and released
to the pleading prayers
bowed and kneeling
within the words
crossed and felt

God and the empty convictions
bleeding the horror
and truth,
a struggle
of perception and means
lonely, the lonely eyes
of wanting
a mirror reflection
is it love?
is it destiny?
or
is it fear?

what you see,
what you see

open, enter
it's not what you know
it's not what the eyes can see
it's love, love unconditionally

it's the birth,
it's the death
reach in,
reach in
are you afraid,

you are not alone
in the quest
for tis in each and everyone
of us
the true running emotion,
it hurts
but it's beautifully real

embrace, enrapture
the feeling
and experience yourself,
within yourself to be

Winter Solace

for the days un-wandering
and streets un-wide
latter day soldiers,
in feast,
the wolf, the media
of masses
pleading innocence
in sheep's clothing
hate and blindness
bleeds on the ringing
song of Christmas
love and light
in through the dark
vastness of the skies

orbs of vision, sink
into the veins
of barbwire crowns
holy is the war,
the war of the faithlessly
departed (souls)
upon the bleeding lands
of covered faces
truth, politics
of blinding faith
a crucifix
of man
human,
greed, jealousy

born in death
and suffering,
from promises
of fortune
and virgin day smiles,
cleansing, penetrating
love,
love and honor

Season's

take a moment and feed yourself
with time, light and freedom
express and expand,
thyself
into the spaciousness,
the beauty and the conversation
that abounds the silence
take hand and give voice
to the unknown,
the dream that's soaring
in your souls abide
do not be afraid
of the darkness of the night
experience it's light
of compelling truth
and inspiring compassion

the two sides of dawn
meet at the corner
half shaded, half alight
upon the two way street
reckoning the passion, the love
between
as death awaits us all
so does life.

The Intangible Heart

O' God
hold me, embrace me
in the wings of your arms
"home"
in the warmth, the spirit
the beauty
of your strength, faith
and grace
murmuring the love
of all you are
in through the face,
the glory of my soul
bless me
please, please
let me feel the pain,
the pain for as I can know,
know the freedom, the peace
respectively and willful
to the admiration
in color and creed
to the humility
the open compassionate self,
self of being
mortal, immortal

the vulnerability
of human suffering
and it's beauty
there of...
you o' Lord
and all,

not the promises,

but of all,
all you've given
inside
the heart and soul
to be
for the choices,
the beauty,
beyond that threshold
of seeing

Christ's Name

smiles of midnight
light the church bells ring
laughter and dreams
among the prayers
sung
in vision
to the day
of Christmas
exchanging the gifts,
words,
feelings
on high
as the spirit
of the season
seeps in the mist
of a starlit night (sky)
beautiful enunciation
in breath and breathing
the slow increments
of time
family and friends
received and given
under the tree
of life
there upon the cross
of divine
love
offered,
opened
and presented

in the birth,
compassionate
and real

a sacrifice
of self
and deliverance
of death upon rebirth

Christ,
within the blood of faith
and touch of compassion
nailed in love
hung in humility

❖ the valley-sunrise
  ❖ death's door

The Valley Sunrise

I've felt death
arise around me
and I've shaken
its darkness
with the light
of faiths welcoming hands
dressed in the disguise
of tempted beauty
I've kissed her
and revealed the truth
on the edge of times
broken promises
long hidden
facing the mirror
in the moment of fate
and the soul
of being
I've seen myself
for the first time
with my own eyes
standing naked, empty and
fulfilled
with the dire of dreams
alive and well
I offer back to you
that same beauty
the same reflection
of yourself to be
in the light

of your own

truth

It's been said you have to go
to the edge
to get to the center
remember the only fear or
danger
is in quitting

Death's Door

tear lights of darkness
beckon the evening's call
awaiting the destiny
of the mornings shadow
knocking at the door

the beginning,
the end

scrolling thee emotion
deep
within
the pain,
and happiness
of the time
present – past

trail winds of memories
seep into the flowering
meadows of life
the smile,
the voice that riddles and rattles
across your own
time, the precious time
we see so hastily,
holds so dear
in the heart, the soul
of weeping
now in the vast narrow reality
of love and life

it's beauty, it's pain

carrying the fever, the absolute spirit
divine ambience
of freedom, awakened
to the light of midnight
and the darkness of noon

a tranquility, a traveling twilight
upon the feast in the palace of souls

❖ the moon's breaking tide
❖ a child's tears
❖ Hannah's smile

*I wrote this poem out of an older version. About the
day my brother passed away, this was on the 8th
anniversary, I sat down upon a bench in the city of
New Haven and reflected back, back into the
memory and presence there of my brother Todd.
And this is that day!*

The Moon's Breaking Tide

silence stood a-graced
upon the door,
in a gazing stare
as the darkness grew
out of the sunlight of day
words were spoken
falling empty with no reply
seeing the vacancy
of my brothers eyes,
the distance found him
as the closeness drew near,
the door that opened
he turned and walked through
entering the exit,
the symmetry of no return
upon separation and the spirits
invocation
present and befriended
calling out in name,
a sadness,
a beauty

touching the warmth
and coldness
of the time
awakened and put to sleep
as I recall that day,
the evening lights suffused into the
continuity
of another...
there amid the questions,
the faith
days on passed, in a dream, I awoke
to the vision,
in soul, in heart
of face
I saw the smile,
the gleam from my brother's eyes

speaking, telling me
he was here to say goodbye,
but only in a physical sense
that he would always be there,
as he gathered us all around,
family,
he said remember this
"I am free, happy and at peace"
do this for me please,
do not cry, do not weep
for me or my life
enter into the spirit,
the happiness with full conviction
each and every day
for this is my wish unto you,

and through that door, I noticed had
changed,
he said goodbye, with some finality
he smiled and crossed its plane
and I awoke, awakened to the breath and
a tear
of bittersweet blessings
of the times, we laughed, bruised and cried
and in knowing the kindness my brother
carried
in his heart
that he had said goodbye to us
upon the will of his way

as I look now and see
as bright as day
his smile
through the door-way
of time,

infinite

This a poem of a young girls struggle with leukemia,
her name is Hannah Pite,

<u>A Child's Tears</u>

across the wavering mass
sunsets and mountain peaks
in curly hair, smiling
a little girl
of innocence
upon the country mile –
stretching beauty
in long winding faith
of what, what is to be
there aloft the mornings dew
of silence
speaking,
time ticks
and time slows
in stillness
of a breath
awakening life and presence
there of...

how precious and dear
the moments can be
drawing the clear blue skies
from the coming storm
over and in
a patience, a love

facilitating the congruent strength
of belief
through the wild, free
and answering depth
of heart and soul
here upon today, tomorrow
blessing the dreams
of a child (Hannah)
within the tears
of her disease
the hands of family, friends
and strangers gather
under the healing wings
of prayers to be...

*This is a very hard poem to embrace, though I never
met this young girl, I found a presence, an ever-
growing connection through such strength and faith.
When I found out that she had passed away, it left me
grave but with a beautiful feeling through what she
left with us all. She touched and smiled upon this
world, thru that darkness she found a light, beauty
and grace.*

Hannah's Smile

out on the edge
thru the hush of willows
beside the rose gardens,
her soft smile,
reflects
deep and traveling
upon a moment
and the times,
the times spent
her beauty drawn
and passionate,
murmuring within
the voice,
the laughter
and the tears,
the tears of a child
whispering, whispering love
in name
o'sweet child, sweet, sweet

child

dancing in the sky,
in the island of our soul
dancing in the sky,
her memory, her presence
sings
a peace, a harmony
on the growing weirs
of time
standing, gathering
in the circles
of our hearts
a cherished life
shortened but ever capturing
the spirit, the essence
there of...

may peace abound
and angels flourish
through all the love
you gave

seeded now
now, within our embrace
o' the sorrow, the pain
you lifted,
through a courage
and a grace
"ever transcending"
life

Hannah Shayne Pite
1/30/99 – 3/15/05
Bend, Oregon

❖ eyes of soul
❖ the tapestry of heart
❖ vision's of...

<u>Eyes of Soul</u>

awaken yourself to the beauty, the thrill
that life

offers and extends

escape the sorrows, relinquish the pain

and enter the blossom,

the blossom of a friend,

friendships divinity

on dawns, dawns

breaking darkness

The Tapestry of Heart

tuesday morning spring
seamlessly spoken
and wed
across the primrose
of my breath
I'm walking here alone
through the pages
of my love
through the pages
of my love
deep in tears
of happiness,
happiness and pain

the sidewalks fill
with faces -
in the sun, the sun
of the city lights
and I dress myself
in the warmth,
the warmth
of a dream
singing a song,
a song of yesterday

the sweet blossom
of her eyes
whisper through,
through the wind

calling on the lips
of my presence
and I can feel the dances
of the night, still beating
in my heart

here I walk alone, alone
through the pages
of my love

the sun burst, through
the sky
clear, blue and bright
to a rhythm
in view
casting the enthrall,

exotically,
to the warming
of my heart,
to the embrace
of my arms

here between the streets,
cars hiss by
the shadows of the builds,
the silhouettes of my dreams
and I,
walk alone
through the pages,
the pages of my love

in reflection of the city,
in reflection
of my soul
as time weaves
thru the screams
of silence
in the conversation
of my life

broken, mused
and secretly impassioned

called forth
and blinded
in beauty, in depth
of ego
and here I walk alone,
alone through the pages,
the pages of my love

Visions of...

There in the morning's meadow of first light

gazing across that horizon of dream

shall I awake unto peace, out of silence

growing in the heart, on the soft colors

stir, of a new day. Where I will be, in the

rapture of beauty, with the love,

the love of life.

This is not thee end, no this is just the beginning.
Open your eyes and feel the touch,
the love of yourself to be, to be alive!!!

Alive and free!

ISBN 141207550-5